SPORTS TIPS, TECHNIQUES, AND STRATEGIES

An Insider's Guide to WRESTLING

NATALIE REGIS AND DAVID CHIU

rosen publishing's rosen central®

NEW YORK

Published in 2015 by The Rosen Publishing Group, Inc. 29 East 21st Street, New York, NY 10010

First Edition

Library of Congress Cataloging-in-Publication Data

Regis, Natalie.
An insider's guide to wrestling / by Natalie Regis and David Chiu.
p. cm. -- (Sports tips, techniques, and strategies)
Includes bibliographical references and index.
ISBN 978-1-4777-8089-3 (library binding)
ISBN 978-1-4777-8090-9 (paperback)
ISBN 978-1-4777-8091-6 (6-pack)
1. Wrestling -- United States -- History -- Juvenile literature. 2. Wrestling -- Juvenile literature. I. Regis, Natalie. II. Title.

GV1195.3 R445 2015
796.812--d23

Manufactured in the United States of America

Metric Conversion Chart			
1 inch	2.54 centimeters 25.4 millimeters	1 cup	250 milliliters
1 foot	30.48 centimeters	1 ounce	28 grams
1 yard	.914 meters	1 fluid ounce	30 milliliters
1 square foot	.093 square meters	1 teaspoon	5 milliliters
1 square mile	2.59 square kilometers	1 tablespoon	15 milliliters
1 ton	.907 metric tons	1 quart	.946 liters
1 pound	454 grams	355 degrees F	180 degrees C
1 mile	1.609 kilometers		

Contents

CHAPTER 1

A History of Wrestling

There is no sport as old as wrestling. It is played when two opponents try to pin or hold each other's shoulders on a mat on the ground. The object is to win by pinning the opponent or by scoring the most points through various maneuvers.

Wrestling is an ancient sport played all over the world.

Prehistoric Wrestling

The oldest form of wrestling dates to prehistoric times, when the sport was a form of hand-to-hand combat. In parts of southern Europe, evidence of wrestling's origins have been found in paintings and carvings in caves. Many of these paintings and carvings are 20,000 years old. Artifacts have also shown that wrestling has been around in several ancient civilizations. An ancient portrait of Sumerian wrestlers on stone slabs, believed to be 5,000 years old, has been found in ancient Mesopotamia.

Paintings depicting wrestling matches dating back to the 20th century BCE have been found in a tomb at Beni Hassan, an ancient Egyptian burial site.

Archeologists found a small bronze statue depicting wrestlers, in the ruins of Khafaji (near present-day Baghdad, Iraq), which dates back to 2600 BCE. In Egypt, walls of temple tombs dating from 2500 BCE show scenes of belt wrestling, an early form of the sport. Aspects of belt wrestling are still used today in modern wrestling.

Plato is an ancient Greek philosopher who contributed to many modern disciplines. He was a successful wrestler in his youth.

Wrestling in Ancient Civilizations

The ancient Greek poet Homer described a wrestling match in the epic poem *The Iliad*. The match between the Greek warriors Odysseus and Ajax ended in a draw. The struggle between these two warriors is considered to be one of the world's greatest wrestling stories.

In ancient Greece, wrestling was introduced to the Olympic Games in 708 BCE. There were two forms of competition in the games: a toppling event for the best two out of three falls, and pankration, a combination of wrestling and boxing. The most famous of ancient wrestlers of that era—Milo of Croton—won the championship six times. But wrestling was not restricted to those blessed with great physical talents. The Greek philosopher Plato (c. 428–348 BCE), then known as Aristocles, was a successful wrestler as a young man.

For a brief time, when the Roman Empire controlled half of Europe in the 100s CE, wrestling's popularity diminished. However, wrestling made a comeback in the Middle Ages (400s–1500s CE). In fact, it became so popular that some nations considered it a noble sport. In England and France, a champion wrestler was highly prized. In 1520, Henry VIII of England and Francis I of France, both supporters of wrestling, challenged each other to a match. Francis I is supposed to have won.

A form of wrestling, called sumo, was developed by the Japanese. It gained popularity during imperial times (710–1185). In 9th-century Japan, the sons of the late emperor Butonku wrestled to determine who would take over the kingdom. Contestants in sumo weighed between 300 and 400 pounds and wrestled in a circle 12 feet in diameter. The goal was to break the opponent down on the mat or pull him out of the ring. Sumo matches were usually over in seconds. These matches are practiced even today.

Sumo wrestling gained popularity during imperial times. It is still practiced in Japan.

Milo of Croton

The 6th-century BCE Greek wrestler Milo of Croton was undefeated in six Olympic championships. How did he condition to hold on to his titles? According to legend, he trained in the off-season for his victories by carrying a newborn calf on his back every day, until it grew into a bull. He was also known for proudly donning his wreaths around his neck as he walked down the streets of his village, to the delight of the townspeople. Unfortunately, though, Milo would die a horrible death: his hand got stuck as he was trying to rip a tree apart. Unfortunately, a pack of wolves attacked and killed him.

This statue, in honor of Milo of Croton, stands at the Louvre in France.

Wrestling in North America

Native Americans practiced wrestling before Europeans began moving to the New World in 1492. This form of the sport had few rules and any hold or leverage could be used to win the match, as long as the opponent was pinned on the ground. By the 16th and 17th centuries, wrestling was a common sport in the colonies of North America. Each settlement had at least one champion wrestler, and contests were held between title holders.

Before becoming president, a young George Washington was a skilled collar and elbow wrestler. Collar and elbow wrestling was a form of wrestling in which each wrestler placed one hand behind his opponent's neck and the other behind his elbow. Later, at the age of forty-seven when he was commander of the Continental army during the American Revolution (1775–1783), he wrestled against various challengers from the Massachusetts Volunteer Infantry.

Future president Abraham Lincoln was a wrestling champion in Illinois around 1830. His approach was catch-as-catch-can, which allowed a wrestler to grab any part of the opponent's body. Wrestling was popular among presidents. Andrew Jackson, Ulysses Grant, and Theodore Roosevelt also enjoyed wrestling.

President George Washington enjoyed wrestling into his late 40s.

Abraham Lincoln, too, was an avid wrestler before he became president.

Greco-Roman Wrestling in Europe

The Greco-Roman style of wrestling developed in France in the mid-1800s. Greco-Roman wrestling does not allow holds on the legs or any form of tripping. Despite it's name, this style of wrestling has nothing in common with the wrestling style of Ancient Greece or Rome. Greco-Roman wrestling was popular in France where public exhibitions were held. However, this style wasn't immediately popular in the United States. The collar and elbow style was practiced by the troops in the Union army during the Civil War (1861–1865). After the war, wrestlers used to travel across the country competing for prize money. The catch-as-catch-can style flourished in the United States in the 1800s.

The Greco-Roman style of wrestling, a popular Olympic sport since 1896, does not allow competitors to touch each other below the waist.

The Modern World and Wrestling

In 1896 wrestling became a part of the modern Olympics in Athens, Greece. Greco-Roman was the only style used and heavyweight was the only class. Freestyle wrestling was introduced in the 1904 Olympic Games in St. Louis, Missouri. Unlike Greco-Roman, freestyle allows holds below the waist and on the legs. Since then, there have been both Greco-Roman and freestyle wrestling in various Olympic weight classes.

Freestyle wrestling allows almost all kinds of moves. Above, you can see the Olympics held in London in 1948.

Organized wrestling took shape in America when the Amateur Athletic Union was formed in 1888. As the governing body of the sport, it established guidelines, rules, and weight classes. The Fédération Internationale des Luttes Associes (FILA), founded in 1912, is the international organization that sets the rules.

The Intercollegiate Wrestling Association was formed in 1903. It was made up of several northeastern universities, such as Yale, Princeton, and Columbia. This association set the rules for college wrestling. Wrestling programs at colleges such as Iowa State University and Oklahoma A&M (now Oklahoma State) soon took off. In 1928, the National Collegiate Athletic Association (NCAA), the governing body of all college sports, held the first wrestling championship tournament. After World War II (1939–1945), wrestling became a standard part of high school and college athletic programs.

Over the years, wrestling has been universally recognized as a major sport because of its exposure in the Olympics, the Pan American Games, and World Championships. These competitions are extremely intense and thrilling as audiences enthusiastically root for their countrymen.

Wrestling is still a popular sport that has many spectators. Above, you can see the final match of the U.S. National Wrestling Championships at the Las Vegas Convention Center.

Women's wrestling has been around since ancient times, even though wrestling has traditionally been a male-dominated sport. It wasn't until the latter part of the 20th century that it became widely accepted through the World Championships of Freestyle Wrestling and the Pan Am Games. In 2001, the women's competition was finally added to the Olympic Games. It made its debut in the 2004 Olympic Games in Athens, Greece.

Female wrestling is also gaining popularity and credibility. These women participate in an exhibition match at the party promoting Paris' bid to host the 2012 Olympic Games.

American amateur wrestling is governed by USA Wrestling (formerly the United States Wrestling Federation). The organization is responsible for the selection and training of the U.S. teams in international competition. USA Wrestling promotes the sport with activities and programs for various age levels. It sanctions more than 1,600 local, state, regional, and national championships; and charters more than 2,900 wrestling clubs.

CHAPTER 2

How to Play

Wrestling can be played by almost anyone. Under wrestling's weight classification system, you compete against someone your own size and weight. Even kids as young as four can wrestle.

Wrestling Styles

There are three types of wrestling at the amateur level: folkstyle, freestyle, and Greco-Roman. Folkstyle is practiced in elementary school through college. It allows the use of arms, legs, and body to hold opponents above or below the waist. Freestyle is very similar to folkstyle but differs in scoring and strategies. It is most popular in North America. In Greco-Roman style, wrestlers are not allowed to grab the legs of their opponents or use any holds below the waist. This style is practiced mostly in Europe. Most national and international competitions, such as the Pan American Games and Olympics, consist of freestyle and Greco-Roman wrestling. The rules in the major tournaments are different compared to those of high school and college, although the moves are the same.

This wrestler attempts to trip his opponent by grabbing his legs.

The Mat

The mat is usually made of foam no more than 4 inches thick and covered in plastic. At the high school level, the mat has a large circle, which is usually 28 feet in diameter. For college competition, the circle on the mat is 32 feet in diameter. The larger circle is the wrestling area. The competition starts at the inner circle, which measures 10 feet in diameter, which is within the larger circle. At the high school level, the inner circle contains parallel starting lines that are 3 feet by 12 inches on the outside. For college, these lines measure 3 feet by 10 inches. This is where the wrestlers begin their match. There is also a 5-foot safety area surrounding the larger circle. Wrestlers have to stay inbounds during play. This means they can't go beyond the boundary lines; if they do, the referee halts the action and tells the wrestlers to return to the center.

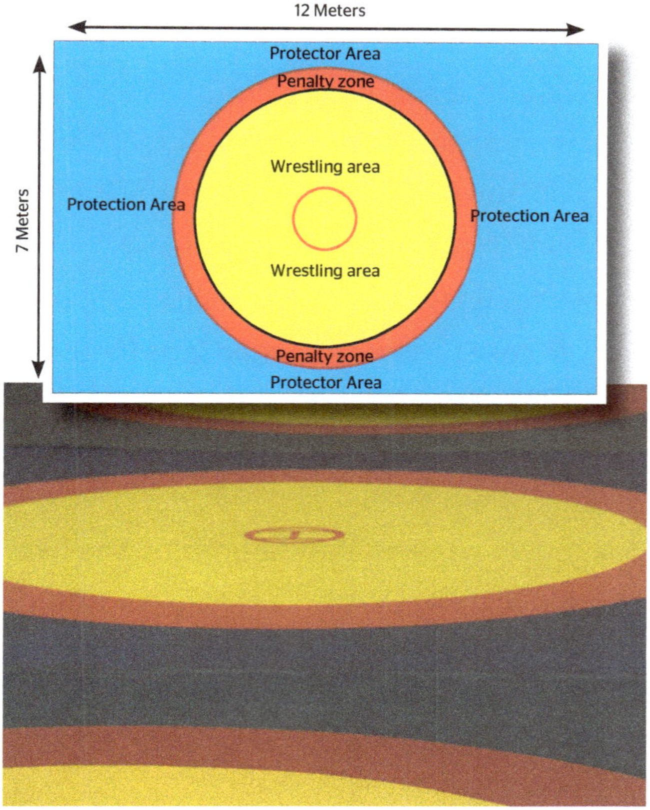

Above is a diagram indicating the boundaries of a wrestling ring.

If a wrestler moves outside the line around the mat, he or she is out-of-bounds. However, the wrestler can score a takedown if his or her feet are inbounds.

The Wrestling Match

A wrestling match takes place on a mat with the two opponents facing each other and a referee to supervise the action. In a wrestling match, unlike in team sports, you are on your own. The main purpose is to use various moves to control your opponent. A wrestling match can be won in two ways. You can hold your opponent's shoulders on the mat for a certain number of seconds. This is called a pin or a fall. You can also win by scoring the most points. The rules for both high school and college competitions are similar. Before the contest begins, the wrestlers must weigh in. The weigh-in is conducted by the referee or an official. Wrestlers from opposing teams in the same weight class are paired up by a random drawing.

In high school, a match is divided into three periods lasting for two minutes each. In college, the first period lasts for three minutes, and the second and third periods last for two minutes each. In the first period, both wrestlers shake hands and begin to take their stances in the neutral position, where neither wrestler is in control. A wrestler's feet should not be touching one another. One foot must be on the starting line and the other foot behind the lead foot. The referee blows the whistle and the action begins. As both wrestlers are on their feet, they engage in hand fighting to knock each other off balance. That is accomplished through early moves such as tie-ups. One wrestler will then go for a takedown, the act of bringing the opponent down to the mat from the standing position. The offensive wrestler will then try to pin the opponent's shoulders on the mat to win the match or score points by holding his opponent on his back.

The defensive wrestler will try to escape and get back to a standing position; if successful, points are awarded. If the defensive wrestler escapes and does a reversal move in which he or she now controls his opponent, he or she gains even more points. The referee will let the official scorer know when points are awarded. The referee marks the end of the first period by sounding the whistle after two minutes (three minutes in college play).

Shown above is a match between Tsabolov, Russia (in red), and Radulov, Ukraine (in blue), at an International freestyle wrestling tournament in Kiev, Ukraine, on February 16, 2013.

The wrestler in red has been brought down by his opponent in blue and is at a disadvantage. He must try to escape and get back to a standing position.

At the beginning of the second and third periods, the wrestlers are in the referee's position. Here the bottom, or defensive wrestler, is on his hands and knees. The knees are also behind the back starting line. The palms are flat on the mat and forward of the front starting line. The top, or offensive wrestler, has one arm around the bottom wrestler's waist with the palm on the opponent's navel. The other hand is over the opponent's elbow.

At the beginning of the second period, a coin toss determines which wrestler has a choice of being in the top, bottom, or neutral position. When the referee blows the whistle to start the second period, the offensive or top wrestler tries to break down the opponent or flatten him or her on the mat. The top wrestler uses whatever breakdown moves or pinning combinations are possible. Like in the first period, the defensive wrestler has to avoid being pinned down on his or her back or either the match will be lost or points will be given up to the opponent. The referee lets the officials know which wrestler scores points. After two minutes, the whistle is blown and the action is halted.

The second wrestler has a choice of the top, bottom, or neutral position at the start of the third period. After the whistle is blown by the referee, the offensive wrestler tries to keep the opponent pinned down, while the defensive player tries to reverse the play by escaping the hold. Points for an escape or reversal are awarded to the defensive wrestler. After two minutes have elapsed, the referee ends the match. If no fall occurs, the match is decided on which wrestler scored the most points. The official scorer notifies the referee of the decision. The wrestlers are brought to the center of the circle to shake hands. The referee then raises the arm of the winner.

Individual Match

In an individual competition, points for individual scores are as follows:

Takedown: 2 points **Escape:** 1 point **Reversal:** 2 points **Near Fall:** 2, 3, or 4 points

Dual Meet

The following are points awarded in a dual meet:

Fall: 6 points **Forfeit:** 6 points **Disqualification:** 6 points **Technical Fall (by more than 15 points):** 5 points **Major Decision:** 4 points **Decision (fewer by 8 points):** 3 points

Wrestling Officials

Several people are responsible for making sure the match goes smoothly and fairly. These are the head referee, the assistant referee, the scorers, and the timekeeper.

The head referee wears a striped black-and-white shirt, black trousers, black gym shoes, and a whistle. This referee's decisions are final based on the rules. Before a match, the head referee will inspect the wrestlers to make sure they are not wearing or carrying any foreign substances or objects that are harmful to the wrestler or the opponent. The decision of what equipment is legal, such

Earl William Hebner is probably the most well-known wrestling referee. He has been a professional wrestling referee since 1988.

as the uniform and the mat, is left to the referee. He or she explains the rules to the coach if necessary. The referee also reviews the procedures with the scorers and the timekeeper.

Decisions such as calling fouls and enforcing penalties are in the hands of the referee.

The head referee enforces penalties for violations and stops illegal holds before they become dangerous. He signals points to the scorers by using his fingers. On his left wrist he wears a red armband, and on his right wrist a green armband. The armbands are used to indicate whether the home or visiting team scored points. At the end of the match, he signs the score book from the scorers to finalize the results.

Sometimes an assistant referee is there to help the head referee. He prevents an error in judgment. However, the head referee still has the final say in a decision.

The official scorer records the points and goes over the scores at the end of the match. If there is a disagreement over the score, the scorer speaks with the timekeeper.

The timekeeper's job is to keep the overall time of the match. He also notifies the referee of a situation when the match is stopped or if there is a disagreement between himself and the scorer.

Scoring in a Match

In both high school and college wrestling, contestants are awarded points for both individual and team competition. With the exception of a pin or fall, in which the wrestler holds the opponent's shoulders for a number of seconds on the mat and thus ends the match, points determine the winner.

Dual Meet

A dual meet is a competition between two teams. Scoring is based on the results of each individual match. For example, if a wrestler pins or falls his opponent, his team gains six points. If he scores more than fifteen points over his opponent, his team receives five points and the match ends in a technical fall.

The wrestler in red is pinned down by his opponent. If he does not break free of the pin, he will lose the match.

There are several situations that can break a tie if both teams have the same score at the end of a dual meet. First, if one team has been penalized more than the other for flagrant misconduct, unsportsmanlike behavior, or stalling, the other team is declared the winner. Second, the team that has the most number of takedowns, reversals, or escapes is declared the winner. Third, the team that won the most matches during the meet is declared the winner.

Wrestling Tournaments

At the end of the season, your team is likely to compete against other schools or wrestling clubs at a tournament. Championships from the school to national level are determined in a tournament. In it, you are likely to wrestle several competitors in one day. A tournament can be very long. In addition to taking a compulsory forty-five minute rest period between two consecutive matches, no one is allowed to compete in more than five matches in one day.

U.S. Army World Class Athlete Program wrestler Sgt. Iris Smith (in blue) defeats China's Lijun Yang (in red) for the Gold in the women's 158.5-pound freestyle division at the 27th World Military Wrestling Championships in Lahti, Finland.

Dremiel Byers waits for the right opportunity to strike at the 2008 London Olympics.

A tournament consists of four, eight, or sixteen teams in a series of individual rounds. A team advances to the final round through either single elimination or double elimination. In a single elimination, two teams face each other in a round. The winning team advances to the next round and plays another winning team, while the losers are automatically eliminated. This continues until only one winner is left. A team has to lose twice before being eliminated in a double elimination.

TNA World heavyweight champion Samoa Joe after a match.

CHAPTER 3

Some Basic Moves

To wrestle, you require strength as well as a keen sense of strategy. Champion wrestlers such as Dave Schultz and John Smith relied on strategy in addition to their physical skills on the mat. To wrestle successfully, you must be able to know how to counterbalance your opponent's attack in addition to being on the offense.

Dwayne Johnson, better known as "The Rock," is one of the most famous wrestlers of all time.

Tie-Ups and Stances

At the start of the first period, the wrestlers shake hands and take their stances at the neutral position. Here, neither wrestler is in control as one faces the other. The stance allows you to be on the defensive and gives you the chance to move. There are two types of stances. In the squared stance, both feet are shoulder-width apart, and neither foot is forward. The staggered stance is similar to the squared stance except that one foot is in front of the other.

The referee sounds the whistle and the match begins. Now both of you will begin to make your move on each other. You should try to distract your opponent and go for a takedown.

An "elbow drop" is a move in which a professional wrestler jumps down on an opponent, driving his or her elbow into the opponent's body, as shown above.

Sgt. David Arendt Jr. (in red) grapples with his opponent, a Russian wrestler, during his second match at the Vantaa Cup Wrestling Tournament in Vantaa, Finland.

One of the preliminary moves in the standing position that can lead to a takedown is called a tie-up.

One kind of tie-up commonly used is the collar tie-up. The collar tie-up with inside arm control involves clamping one hand on the back of the opponent's neck while using the other hand to grab the inside of the opponent's arm.

Lifting

Lifting an opponent is an important skill as it distracts your opponent and makes him or her vulnerable. As you drive into your opponent, bend at the knees and lower your hips. Make sure you are under your opponent while grabbing him or her by the arms. Then straighten up and hoist your opponent into the air. Using your back to do this can cause you serious injury. The weight should be borne by your legs, hips, and thighs.

Takedowns

In a takedown, you bring your opponent down to the mat and control him or her. If the takedown is done successfully, you are awarded two points. If you score first, you will have a psychological edge throughout the match. Takedowns involve dropping to your hips and taking an aggressive forward step toward your opponent's abdominal area. Simultaneously, keep your chin up and your back straight.

This player (in orange) manages to takedown his opponent (in blue) in a Greco-Roman wrestling match.

One of the most common takedowns is done with a single leg. Here you shoot in low toward your opponent and wrap your arms around his or her leg. Then lift it into the air to get him or her off balance and drive your opponent onto the mat.

When you successfully perform a takedown on your opponent, you can try pinning him or her for the automatic win. The referee blows his whistle, ending the first period if no pin or fall occurs.

Breakdowns

As discussed earlier, the second and third periods begin with the wrestlers in the referee's position. The defensive wrestler is on the bottom and the offensive wrestler is on top. The object for you as the top wrestler is to break down, or flatten, the opponent on his or her stomach or side. To do so, apply pressure to where your opponent has support, such as the hands or feet.

One popular breakdown is the cross-face, far-ankle breakdown, in which you place your left hand across your opponent's face to grasp his or her upper right arm. Grab your opponent's right ankle with the other hand and pull him or her toward you and over onto his or her shoulder.

Spc. Mark Bradley (in red) of the All Army Wrestling team performs a cross-face, far-ankle breakdown to bring his opponent (in blue) down.

Pinning: Cradles and Nelsons

Seize the opportunity to pin your opponent as soon as you have control over him or her on the mat. Pinning is the ultimate way to win a match. In order to win, both of your opponent's shoulder blades must touch the mat for two seconds. If this is not possible, you can also score points in a near fall. This occurs when your opponent's shoulders or scapulas are held within 4 inches of the mat and at an angle of 45 degrees or less. If accomplished for two seconds, you are awarded two points. You are awarded three points if you hold the shoulders four inches off the mat for five seconds.

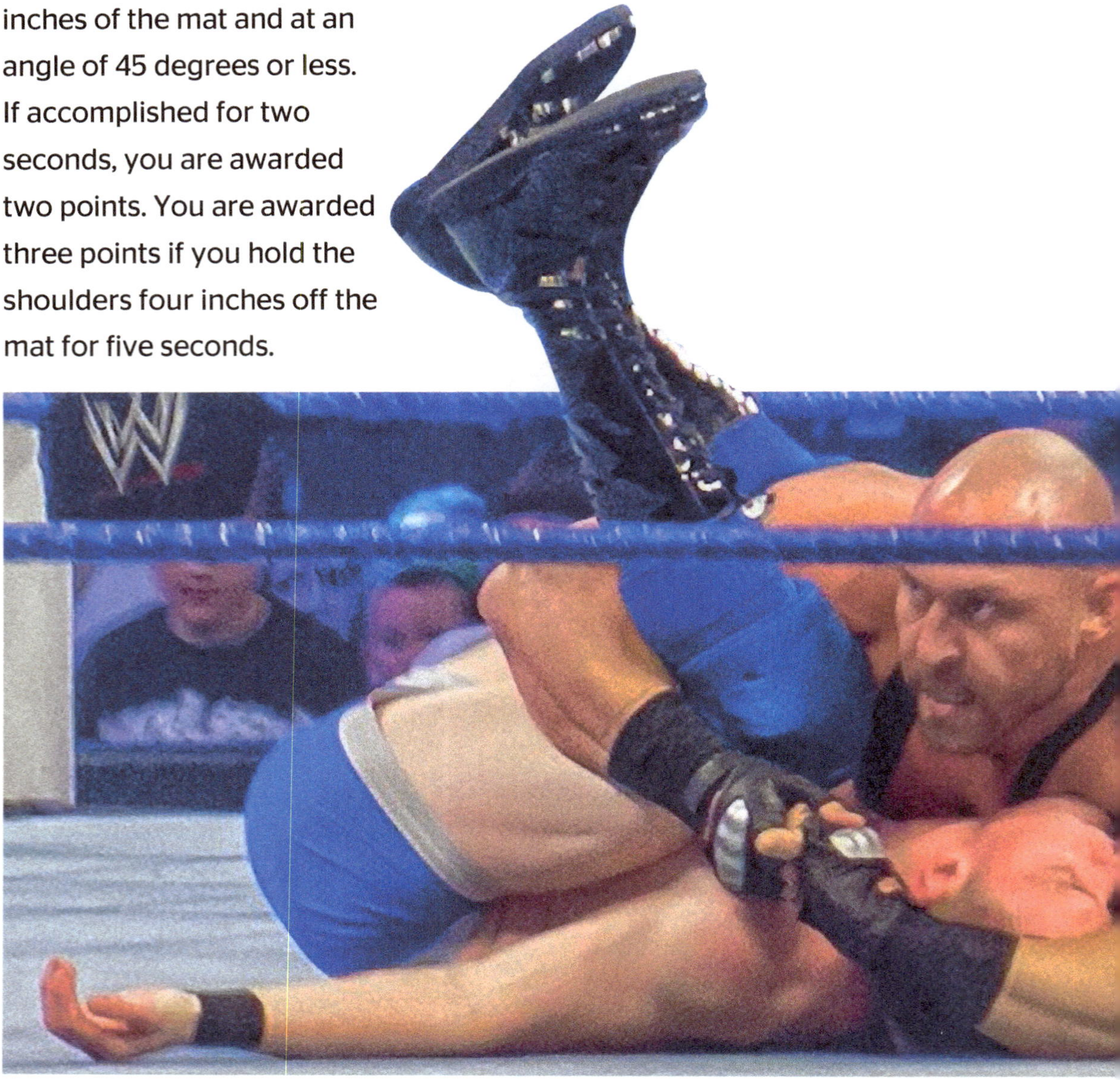

Ryback performs a cradle and pins Jobber during a WWE house show in London in 2012.

You might perform a nelson in one of your pinning moves. A nelson is a hold in which one hand is placed on your opponent's neck by reaching under one or both of his or her arms. You can use the half nelson if your opponent is flat on his or her stomach. Get your left hand under your opponent's left armpit and across the back of his or her neck. Hold tight your opponent's right hand with your right hand to prevent an escape. Swing your body perpendicular to his or hers and drive your legs in so you end up chest to chest with your opponent.

Cradles are maneuvers useful in pinning. One example is the near-side cradle in which you place your left arm across your opponent's neck. Then use your right hand and place it under his or her left knee. Lock hands and drive your head into your opponent's ribcage while lifting his or her other knee, and force your opponent onto his or her back.

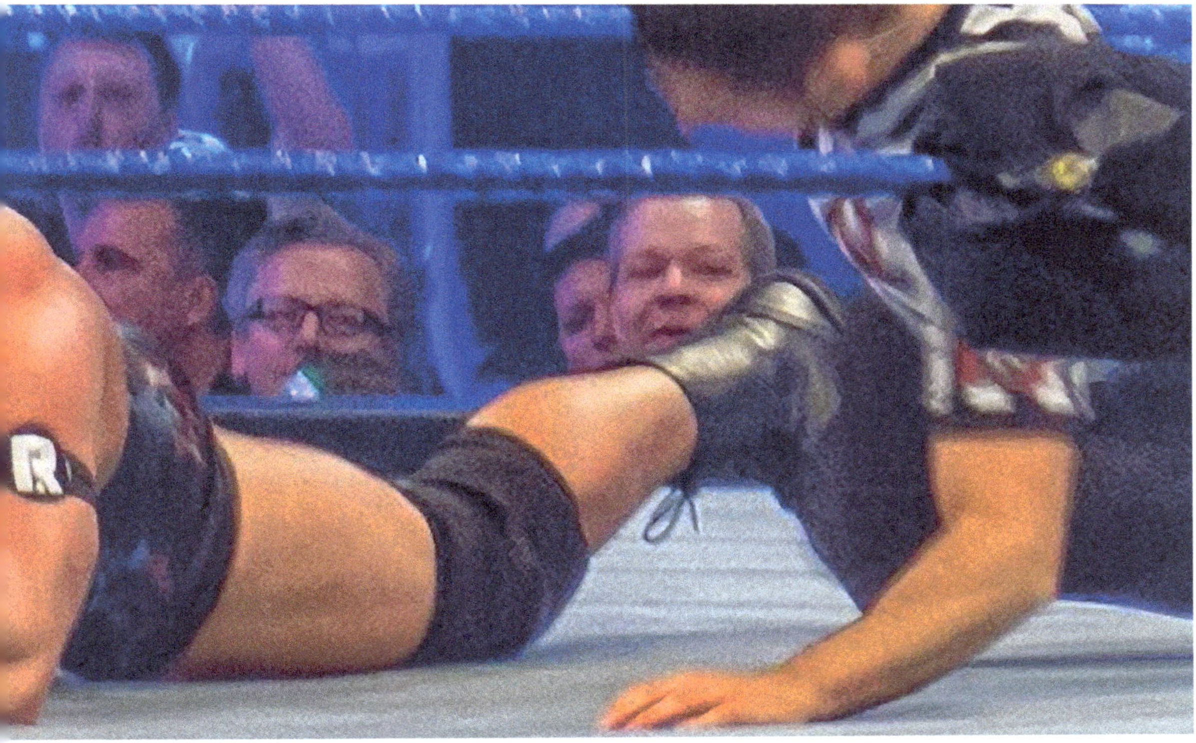

Escapes

Being able to escape from your opponent can be the difference between winning and losing. An escape, worth one point, is a move in which you are able to free yourself and get back into the neutral position. A reversal is a move in which you switch from the bottom position to the top position. You go from being controlled by to controlling your opponent. If the move is done successfully, you are awarded two points.

US Marine Sergeant Brian Van Hoven tries to escape from George Moustopoulos, from Greece, during the 132 lb Free-Style 19th World Military Wrestling Championship on October 29, 2000.

One way to escape is to execute the stand-up. Shift your weight into your opponent's body and grab your opponent's left wrist with your right hand as you try to get up. Lock elbows so your opponent can't reach in under your arms. Get up on your left foot in front of your right leg and thrust your entire body upward. Use your hands to free your waist from your opponent's hand.

Infractions and Illegal Holds

Like all other sports, in order to prevent injuring yourself or your opponent, you must follow certain rules. You can lose points or be disqualified if they are not followed.

Certain holds on the mouth, nose, throat, or neck that restrict breathing or circulation are banned. Some examples include the full nelson, body slams, and strangleholds. The first and second penalties are worth one point each, the third penalty is worth two points, and the fourth penalty carries a disqualification.

Stalling is another violation. It occurs when a wrestler is intentionally wasting time by staying out of bounds, playing at the edge of the mat, or not attempting to wrestle. In college matches, the offending wrestler will receive a warning after the first violation, and will be penalized a point for the second and third time it occurs. After a two-point penalty for the fourth violation, he or she will be disqualified from the match if called for a fifth time.

Unsportsmanlike conduct is not tolerated. Examples include ignoring the referee's warnings and shoving, taunting, swearing, and intimidating your opponent. Flagrant misconduct includes biting, striking, and kicking an opponent. The wrestler will be removed from the premises and his team will lose points if the referee considers the misconduct to be serious.

US Marine Corps Corporal Jacob Clark (in blue) is pinned by his opponent during the Armed Forces Wrestling Championship held in New Orleans, Louisiana.

A wrestler is not permitted to continue the match if he or she injures his or her opponent using an illegal hold, and the injured wrestler wins by default. If a wrestler intentionally injures the opponent, the wrestler will be disqualified. If a wrestler is accidentally injured and cannot carry on, his or her opponent wins.

Great Wrestlers

The National Wrestling Hall of Fame and Museum, located in Stillwater, Oklahoma, was founded in 1976. It honors the greatest wrestlers in the sport and houses memorabilia from wrestling's past. Here are a few great wrestlers and some of their career highlights.

Dan Gable had a combined prep and college record of 181 wins and 1 loss. His greatest moment was at the 1972 Olympics in Munich, Germany, where he defeated all six opponents without giving up a single point.

Dave Schultz collected ten national championships. He won an Olympic gold medal in 1984 by defeating his opponents with a combined score of 42 to 2.

Bruce Baumgartner had a record of 134 wins and 12 losses, including pinning his opponents 73 times in his college career. He would go on to become World Champion in 1986, 1993, and 1995. In the 1984 Olympics, Bruce became the first American in 60 years to win a gold medal in the super heavyweight class.

John Smith became known for his quick single-leg takedown that made him unstoppable. His combined career record was a winning rate of more than 95 percent, with 436 wins, 20 losses, and 2 ties.

Rulon Gardner's Greco-Roman wrestling accomplishments included capturing the Pan American championship and Vantaa cup in 1998, and winning the World Cup in 1996. His greatest win was defeating the legendary wrestler Aleksandr Karelin of Russia in the 2000 Olympics. It had been thirteen years since Karelin had lost a match and ten years since he had given up a point.

Sgt. Dremiel Byers, a member of the U.S. Army World Class Athlete Program, pins down Olympic gold medalist Rulon Gardner at the U.S. National Wrestling Championships in 2004.

CHAPTER 4

Preparation, Equipment, and Involvement

You do not need much equipment for wrestling. You can start out by wearing gym clothes and sneakers. As you progress in your training and participate in competitions, you will need some special gear. Most sporting goods stores and websites sell wrestling clothes and equipment.

The Clothes

A wrestler wears a singlet, a one-piece, close-fitting nylon uniform that extends from the shoulders to the thighs. Singlets are usually worn during tournaments. Much like uniforms in other sports, the singlet comes in colors representing the wrestler's school or organization.

A singlet is used in amateur wrestling. It is tight-fitting so it cannot be grabbed by an opponent.

Light shoes, like these, help the wrestler be more agile.

The Shoes

Wrestling shoes should be lightweight and reach up to the ankle. They should be rubber soled and heelless, and should have some form of traction. Good wrestling shoes provide flexibility, stability, and support for quick maneuvers.

Ear Guards or Headgears

It is necessary to wear headgear and ear guards during competitions and practice. This is for protection of the ears, where injuries are most common. Cushioned ear cups are held in place by a buckle-free strap to prevent a ruptured ear drum.

Ear guards, like these, provide protection for the delicate ears.

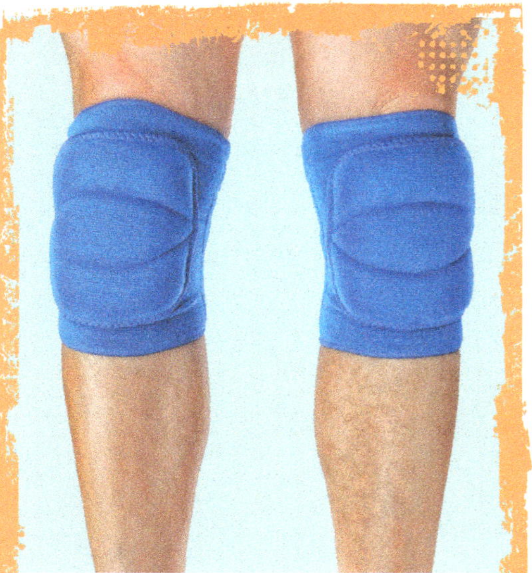

It is advisable to wear knee pads, though it is not compulsory.

The Knee Pads

Wearing knee pads is optional, although they offer protection against getting bruised, worn knees.

Weight Requirements

All competitors must weigh in before a wrestling match begins to ensure fairness of competition. The weights are recorded by the official scorer. Afterward, the contestants in the same weight classification are paired through a random draw. In high school wrestling has fourteen different weight classes, ranging from 103 pounds to 275 pounds. For college competitions, the weight classes vary from 125 pounds to 183 to 285 pounds.

Rapid Weight Loss is Dangerous

Some wrestlers feel pressure to lose weight so that they can stay within their proper weight class and gain an edge. Some wear a rubber suit to sweat and, therefore, shed pounds. Some employ extreme means, such as starving themselves or vomiting. Drugs and nutritional supplements have also been used as weight loss aids. All these methods are illegal and very dangerous to the health of a wrestler. Excessive weight loss leads to tiredness, mood swings, short-term memory loss, and even death. In 1997, three college wrestlers died trying to meet weight requirements for competition. You should consult your doctor or nutritionist on how to maintain your ideal weight.

Nutrition for Aspiring Wrestlers

As in any sport, wrestling requires that you eat the right foods. A well-balanced diet ensures good physical and mental health. According to a study by the Center for Nutrition in Sport and Human Performance conducted for the NCAA, this consists of foods containing the following:

Carbohydrates make up for lost energy burned during play, and they stimulate muscle growth. Foods rich in carbohydrates include potatoes, cereal, bread, pasta, and fresh fruit. Your intake of carbohydrates should be about 60 percent of your total caloric intake.

Fats from sources like soybean oil, olive oil, and canola oil also provide a source of energy. 20 to 30 percent of your calorie intake should comprise of good fats.

Proteins are the essential building blocks of blood, skin, hair, tissues, and muscles. Proteins can be found in foods such as meat, fish, skimmed milk, poultry, and legumes. A normal diet should consist of about 20 percent protein.

Minerals such as calcium and iron are also essential in maintaining good health. Calcium keeps your bones strong. Foods such as leafy green vegetables (spinach, kale) and milk contain calcium. Iron maintains the healthy red blood cells that carry oxygen to your body. Meat, fish, fruits, and greens are rich in iron.

Water is essential before, during, and after play. When you wrestle, you sweat, and your body loses water. Before practice, you should drink about 20 ounces of water every two hours. During practice, you should drink 8 ounces of water every 15 to 20 minutes.

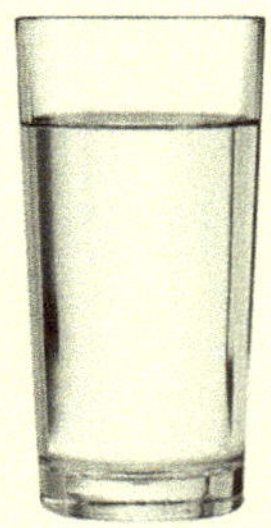

Conditioning and Training

Push-ups help increase upper body strength.

Your body gains strength and you are likely to be healthier if you follow a good conditioning program. Stretching your upper and lower body loosens the muscles, lubricates the joints, and gets the blood flowing. It also decreases your chance for serious injury and discomfort during play. According to Nick Ugoalah, fitness trainer and Canadian free style champion, wrestlers need to spend between ten and fifteen minutes warming up. Such warm-up exercises include running, skipping rope, or using a stair climber. They should be followed by basic stretches for the lower and upper parts of your body. Stretching exercises for the lower portion of your body should include the hamstrings, quadriceps, groin, and calf muscles. These involve holding a part of your leg for about a minute to get a good stretch and then working on the other leg. Upper-body stretches for your arms and back should involve arm circles, push-ups, sit-ups, and pull-ups. Start off with a few repetitions of these and gradually increase them.

Lifting weights also helps wrestlers increase their strength and muscle power.

You must also train with weights as it helps build muscle strength and mass. At your gymnasium or fitness club, you can find weight-training equipment such as free weights, dumbbells, and nautilus machines. Younger children who have not reached puberty should not weight train strenuously because it can harm their skeletal development. If you use the weights properly, you will avoid sprains and injury.

Involvement in other sports and physical activities, or cross training, is beneficial. It will strengthen your muscles while improving your hand-eye coordination and mobility.

Before taking on any rigorous strength and conditioning program, have a checkup from your doctor. Also talk to fitness instructors about what program is suitable for your body.

Getting Involved

You can start wrestling at an early age. Many schools across the country offer wrestling as part of high school sports. There are also youth wrestling clubs and camps that offer individual and group instruction.

Many schools also offer wrestling programs.

One way to introduce yourself to the sport is by watching a wrestling match on television, such as the Olympics. There are also instructional videos that describe the methods and techniques used. These videos can be found at a library or online.

Attending a wrestling match is another way to build your interest in the sport. Find out if your school, college, or local athletic club has wrestling practices and matches. You can learn a lot by observing how the match is conducted and studying the types of moves used. Talk to coaches and wrestlers to get a feel for what competing is like.

If you want to participate in wrestling, find out which organizations and schools in your area have wrestling programs. Contact your library, consult your phone book, or go online to see if there is a wrestling club for kids. If you are fourteen years or older, contact the National Federation of State High School Associations (NFHS), the governing body of high school athletics, to find out which high schools in your state have a wrestling program. You can also contact USA Wrestling for information on sanctioned wrestling associations and clubs in your state.

Wrestling Camps

If you cannot find a local youth or high school level wrestling program in your area, you may want to consider traveling to an overnight youth camp. There are many wrestling camps all over the United States, including programs

It is essential to stretch for at least ten to fifteen minutes before a wrestling match to avoid muscle pulls.

for women. Most camps held during the summer last between a few days to a week. Some former stars like Bruce Baumgartner run their own camps, bringing their unique styles to aspiring wrestlers.

To find out about wrestling camps in your area, consult the phone book or library. Most wrestling camps have websites. Contact USA Wrestling to find certified and recommended camps.

Beyond College

At some colleges, particularly in the Midwest, wrestling is a major part of the athletic programs. Institutions such as Iowa State, Oklahoma State, and the University of Nebraska traditionally have championship wrestling teams that compete for the NCAA title. Depending on athletic ability and academic skill,

Olympic gold medalist, Rulon Gardner, has a chat with aspiring wrestlers from Edgren High School in 2002.

some schools offer wrestling scholarships. College wrestling coaches scout and recruit high school athletes that show promise for their programs.

Beyond college, amateur wrestlers compete in national championships, such as the USAW Senior Freestyle Championships, and international tournaments, such as the World Championships and the Olympics. To participate in the World Championships and the Olympics as a representative of the United States, competitors have to be sponsored by USA Wrestling. In order to qualify to be on the U.S. Olympic team, you must attend tryouts. Spots are won through competition. Even 2000 Olympic gold medalist Rulon Gardner had to earn his place on the 2004 team.

Wrestling is a demanding sport that requires a strong work ethic, endurance, and energy. Although physical strength is very important, being clever and smart can help you get an edge over your opponent. Unlike other sports, wrestling doesn't require much equipment, additional players, or being six feet tall and huge. It is a safe and fun activity that builds self-esteem and confidence, promotes health and fitness, and fosters a competitive spirit. It is the sense of one-on-one competition and overcoming adversity that makes wrestling an appealing and enduring sport. You can become a successful wrestler if you have a good understanding of the techniques and are willing to work hard.

Rulon Gardner and Sgt. Dremiel Byers wrestle against each other for the Gold at the U.S. National Wrestling Championship in 2004.

Glossary

breakdown A move in which the offensive wrestler flattens his or her opponent on his or her stomach or side.

cradle A maneuver that sets up for a pin in which one wrestler wraps his or her arms on the back of the opponent's neck and legs and then locks his or her hands.

fall To hold your opponent on his or her back with both of his or her shoulders touching the mat for two seconds.

folkstyle A style of wrestling practiced from elementary school to college in which opponents are permitted to use their arms, legs, and bodies to secure holds to either win by a pin or by scoring points.

freestyle A style of wrestling, similar to folkstyle, in which opponents are permitted to use their arms, legs, and bodies to secure holds to either win by a pin or by scoring points, though different in scoring and strategy.

Greco-Roman wrestling A style of wrestling in which the wrestlers are not allowed to use their legs during the action.

leverage The use of force in a manner similar to a lever.

maneuver A movement or series of movements requiring skill and care.

pin The act of holding your opponent's shoulders on the mat for two seconds to win the match.

singlet A close-fitting spandex or nylon one-piece uniform worn by wrestlers.

sumo A type of Japanese wrestling.

For More Information

National Federation of State High School Associations (NFHS)
P.O. Box 690
Indianapolis, IN 46206
Website: http://www.nfhs.org

National Wrestling Hall of Fame and Museum
405 W. Hall of Fame
Stillwater, OK 74075
(405) 377-5243
Website: http://nwhof.org/

United States Olympic Committee
National Headquarters
One Olympic Plaza
Colorado Springs, CO 80909
(719) 866-4618
Website: http://www.teamusa.org/

USA Wrestling
6155 Lehman Drive
Colorado Springs, CO 80918
Website: http://www.themat.com/newusaw

Websites

Due to the changing nature of Internet links, the Rosen Publishing Group, Inc., has developed an online list of websites related to the subject of this book. This site is updated regularly. Please use this link to access the list:

http://www.rosenlinks.com/sportscoasttocoast/wrestling

For Further Reading

Black, Jake. *The Ultimate Guide to WWE.* New York, NY: Grosset & Dunlap, 2011.

Cejudo, Henry. *Wrestling For Dummies.* Hoboken, NJ: For Dummies, 2012.

Johnson, Dennis A. *Wrestling Drills For The Mat And Mind.* Cuyahoga Falls, OH: Momentum Media, 2011.

Johnson, Steven. *The Pro Wrestling Hall of Fame: Heroes & Icons (Pro Wrestling Hall of Fame Series).* Toronto, Canada: ECW Press, 2012.

Kreidler, Mark. *Four Days to Glory: Wrestling with the Soul of the American Heartland.* New York, NY: Harper Collins, 2007.

Luger, Lex. *Wrestling with the Devil: The True Story of a World Champion Professional Wrestler - His Reign, Ruin, and Redemption.* Winter Park, FL: Tyndale Momentum, 2013.

Scheff, Matt. *Pro Wrestling Superstars.* Fort Wayne, IN: Sportszone, 2014.

Shoemake, David. *The Squared Circle: Life, Death, and Professional Wrestling.* New York, NY: Gotham, 2013.

Snowden, Jonathan. *Shooters: The Toughest Men in Professional Wrestling.* Toronto, Canada: ECW Press, 2012.

Welker, William. *Wrestling Drill Book.* Champaign, IL: Human Kinetics, 2012.

Bibliography

Dellinger, Bob. "The Oldest Sport." National Wrestling Hall of Fame and Museum. Retrieved April 14, 2014 (http://www.wrestlinghalloffame.org).

Dellinger, Bob. "Wrestling in the USA." National Wrestling Hall of Fame and Museum. Retrieved April 14, 2014 (http://www.wrestlinghalloffame.org).

Diehl, Jerry L., ed. 2003-2004 *NFHS Wrestling Rules Book*. Indianapolis: NFHS Publications, 2003.

Gable, Dan. "Wrestling." *World Book Encyclopedia*. Chicago: World Book, 2003.

Linde, Barbara. *Olympic Wrestling*. New York: Rosen Publishing, 2007.

Periello, Vito. A., M.D. "Aiming for a Healthy Weight in Wrestlers and other Athletes." *Contemporary Pediatrics*, September 2001, pp. 55–74.

Ryan, Thomas, and Julie Sampson. *Beginning Wrestling*. New York: Sterling, 2002.

St John, Chris. Wrestling. New York: Rosen Publishing, 2012.

"Wrestling." Encyclopedia Britannica. 2003. Retrieved April 14, 2014 (http://search.eb.com/eb/article?eu=79631).

Index

Index

About the Authors

Natalie Regis is a writer living in Knoxville, Tennessee. She is a fan of professional wrestling and played the sport in High School in addition to baseball and hockey. In college she rowed crew.

David Chiu is a writer living in New York. He has written several nonfiction books for young people.

Photo Credits

The photographs in this book are used by permission and through the courtesy of: Cover photo by: Lilyana Vynogradova/shutterstock.com, 1; back cover: © Haslam Photography/shutterstock.com; © Tomas Fritz/shutterstock.com; © Baronb/shutterstock.com; © aquariagirl1970/shutterstock.com; © Ryanjo/commons.wikimedia.org; © DeanHarty/shutterstock.com; © Micha Klootwijk/shutterstock.com; © Tomas Fritz/shutterstock.com, 3, 16, 30, 34: © Everett Collection/shutterstock.com, 4; © Dbachmann/commons.wikimedia.org, 4; © Georgy Markov/shutterstock.com, 5; © J. Henning Buchholz/shutterstock.com, 6; © Zyankarlo/shutterstock.com, 6; © thatsmymop/shutterstock.com, 7; © w:en:Centpacrr/commons.wikimedia.org, 7; © Lilyana Vynogradova/shutterstock.com, 8; © National Media Museum/File Upload Bot (Magnus Manske)/commons.wikimedia.org, 9; © Wikiman86/commons.wikimedia.org, 10, 12, 15, 24, 28, 29, 31; © David.Monniaux/commons.wikimedia.org, 11; © Diego Barbieri/shutterstock.com, 13; © PKDirector/shutterstock.com, 13; © Lilyana Vynogradova/shutterstock.com, 14; © KnightNephrite/Maurilbert/commons.wikimedia.org, 17; © testing/shutterstock.com, 18; © Dreier Carr from USA/Wikiman86/commons.wikimedia.org, 19; © U.S. Army/File Upload Bot (Magnus Manske)/commons.wikimedia.org, 20; © Simon/FlickreviewR/commons.wikimedia.org, 21; © Tabercil/ Starship.paint/commons.wikimedia.org, 22; © Slick-o-bot/commons.wikimedia.org, 23, 25; © Ed Webster/Starship.paint/commons.wikimedia.org, 26, 27; © Andrey_Kuzmin/shutterstock.com, 32, 35; © Vladyslav Starozhylov/shutterstock.com, 32; © Sergio Stakhnyk/shutterstock.com, 33; © Nicholas Piccillo/shutterstock.com, 33; © Africa Studio/shutterstock.com, 34, 35; © Robyn Mackenzie/shutterstock.com, 34, 35; © holbox/shutterstock.com, 36; © Monkey Business Images/shutterstock.com, 36; © SUSAN LEGGETT/shutterstock.com, 37; © Matanya/commons.wikimedia.org, 38; © BotMultichillT/commons.wikimedia.org, 39.